I0059826

New Leader Primer

I'm responsible for others, now what? !!

A *simple.transparent.uncluttered*® primer for new leaders with actionable ideas to get moving and stay on track!

Kathleen Winter

Winter Consulting Publishers
Aguanga, CA © 2016
Copyright 2016 All Rights Reserved ©
ISBN: 978-0-578-18635-1

TABLE OF CONTENTS

Introduction   1

Chapter One   6

Chapter Two   17

Chapter Three   24

Chapter Four   36

Chapter Five   49

Remember   52

Recommended Reading

INTRODUCTION

You are reading this book probably for one or several of the reasons listed below:

- You were promoted because your exceptional technical skills stand out and the company was growing.
- Your team got bigger, you were the informal leader and the company was growing.
- You have some experience in supervising others but could use some perspective about how to keep it all together.
- You are an experienced leader, but you and your

team are not delivering

expectations and you don't

know how to turn it around.

But, whatever the reason the
important one is that you are!

In my twenty five years in the
corporate world, in diverse industries
and diverse roles, I experienced and
observed the struggles of first time
supervisors transitioning from being a
doer to a network builder, staying
focused on their team and the
tremendous impact front line
supervisors can have on the success of
the organization. I saw their individual
struggle with not being recognized any
longer for their contribution but their
teams' contribution. I saw experienced

leaders lose focus on the fundamentals during challenging and changing business environments, which resulted in poor team performance that resulted in termination, role eliminations or organizational realignments. The fundamentals to a successful transition apply to all industries and management structures.

My purpose for writing this book is to share a *simple..transparent..uncluttered*® approach on how to make a successful transition from being a doer (individual contributor) to a network builder (manager and leader) that embraces the rewarding opportunity to engage others and lead them on a path of rewards and fulfillment.

The concepts and suggestions covered in this book are not new. There are many leadership, self-help and communication books you can read along with the many on line articles, but in this book I provide concise, simple tactical tools that are immediately actionable along with real life examples of the journey you are beginning.

I've included concepts and references to books that have influenced me and other colleagues on our journey and you will see these references throughout this book. These authors have impacted how I think about leadership, how my actions impact others and through sharing some of their concepts in this book, their principles continue to impact new leaders.

Keep this book handy. Write in the margins, highlight what resonates with you and keep visible to you those phrases that you connect with as a reminder during your life-changing journey of leading others!

Chapter One
No Longer All About You

transitioning from player to team captain and to coach

I love using sports analogies when coaching new managers, new leaders or even experienced leaders for that matter. Most of the time my clients have either played some type of team sport, have a favorite sports team or someone they know spends their Saturdays and Sundays consumed by the sport in season. Even golf and tennis have analogies that are relevant to being an effective leader. Sports, whether played or viewed, can be a rewarding emotional experience that challenges our sense of who we are, what work we are willing to do and how the win or loss can impact others and ourselves.

Throughout my business career it became evident to me that like sports, business had players, team captains and coaches. The "titles" were a bit different but the fundamentals of the game and business were very much alike. As I moved through positions in the corporate world I saw the similarities.

The similarities look like this:
- Know your market and customer (opposing team and fans).
- Have a strategic plan (what game plays need to

occur to win.

- Focus on the fundamentals of your market and customer
- Have the right people in the right roles who are committed and engaged and treat them well (team players and culture).
- Plan for the win (teach the game plays to all players).

Understand and embrace your place on the team and inspire others to success!

Know your position and play it!

Consider the various roles in an organization—where you are today and where you want to be. Focus on mastering the fundamentals of each position you and your team play in order to win the game. There are three different types of positions, so know the one you are in and what it will take to get you to the next one. The positions are:

Player / (individual contributor)

Fundamentals

- Excels in fundamental and technical skills for the position
- Rewarded for personal performance/personal metrics
- Responsible only for yourself
- Plays well with others

If you are an individual contributor in business you are in control of yourself, how you interact with others and your brand in the organization or team.

Team captain (supervisor/manager)

Fundamentals

- Responsible for the team first
- Executing the plays through trust, influence, collaboration
- Responsible for creating an effective development plan for each team member
- Be the newscaster for the team- strategize, influence and inform the team outcomes and value to the organization
- Continue your personal development

If you are a lead, supervisor, or

manager, your first responsibility is to your team. Not only are you responsible for yourself, but also you are responsible for the actions, outcomes and development of the team.

Coach / (leader)

Fundamentals

- Responsible for the team first
- Vision and strategies
- Values and cultural tone
- Alignment of people for maximum outcome

Coaches are always present for the team players, not only physically but also emotionally.

```
          ┌──────────┐
          │   team   │
          │ captain  │
          └──────────┘
               │
               ▼
┌──────────┐        ┌──────────┐
│  player  │ ──►  ◄── │  coach   │
└──────────┘  ╭────╮  └──────────┘
             │ team │
              ╰────╯
```

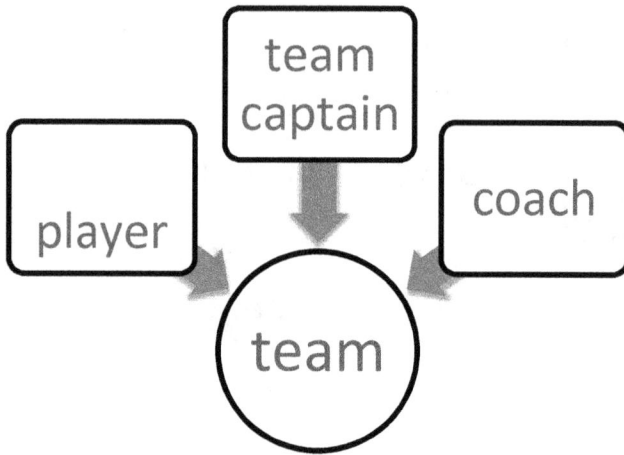

*Play your position and embrace the role and
contribution of others.*

In Marshall Goldsmith's book "*What
Got You Here, Won't Get You There,*"
he shares with his readers the

message that as your roles change throughout your career so do the competencies. Be willing to seek out what those competencies are and start your personal development early. Being forward looking while taking care of business in the moment is one of the keys to success.

In my finance role at a major technology company, I was a business partner to an extremely smart and successful engineer who had been promoted very quickly but his career progression had become stagnant. He had been recruited after attending a prestigious engineering school and had exceptional military experience. His profile was like many in the organization that was growing quickly and he "fit." During his first few years, he was promoted at lightning speed based on executing critical projects for the company, demonstrating exceptional intellectual horsepower and successfully leading others who were like him. But the higher up the promotion ladder he went, he used what he knew to stay on the track. His struggle of connecting with others who were not like him and engaging across functional areas became evident to his leaders.

So, his leader assigned him to a role that would provide him the opportunity to develop competencies that would "get him there." But he was failing, and miserably. During one of our heartfelt conversations about missing a cost target, he revealed he knew he was failing in this new assignment and was clear that the next promotion would only come if he learned to connect and inspire a wide range of people, who were not like him. So, as Dr. Phil says, acknowledging there is a problem is the first step to resolution. I'm happy to conclude by the time he left the organization, the team he led was one of the most diverse, sought after talent in the company and he learned it wasn't about him. Today he is a very successful managing partner of a private equity company.

As you take this journey in your professional and personal life, get comfortable with the fundamentals and competencies that are required at each level. Each role in business or sports is important and requires skill in order to win the game. Embrace and understand the role you have and the role you want! If you are a lead, supervisor, manager or leader remember it is team first and no longer about you!

Chapter Two

Practical Approaches

simple.transparent.uncluttered.

I'm a firm believer in a *simple.transparent.uncluttered.* approach to managing and leading for outcomes. The strength of a team and their outcomes require all players to understand the game strategy, play their position, execute the play and adjust when necessary. So, as the leader you are responsible for making sure the entire team is ready.

The concept of *simple.transparent.uncluttered.* is:

simple.

Think about how to influence and reward the team for simplicities in solving business challenges. You see, teams have varying levels of expertise; various levels of business acumen and can develop group thinking if there is no diversity.

The simplicity approach is not about developing solutions to the lowest common denominator—it is about developing solutions that all team members can participate in and influence outcomes. Don't allow unnecessary complexity that can drive exclusion.

Maximum participation and

understanding can bring focus on a goal, aligned energy and game changing results.

Some examples of simplicity are:

- Define relevant metrics - fewer are better – keep the calculation simple
- Learn to tell the story simply and with one slide
- Keep meetings focused on purpose and don't allow topic hijack

transparent.

I have used the saying, "we all know what we all know" many times. I first heard this saying when implementing a S&OP process in an industry that was unfamiliar to me. I made an assumption on the level of business acumen of the core team and quickly realized, through the guidance of a very wise consultant that "we don't all know, what we don't all know." Once I understood and recognized the challenge, the path forward was less bumpy. The lesson for me was to be as transparent as possible through sharing the end game of this business process and to communicate with the team the newly learned terminology.

However, transparency also means sharing with integrity what you know about a situation or your understanding, and being confident enough to raise your hand when you don't understand. There are many business stories where transparency was not an organization value and consumers, investors and employees were adversely impacted. Search stories on Enron, Countrywide Mortgage, BP, the recent GM ignition scandal and the Takata air bag scandal. Transparency doesn't mean violate privacy laws or openly share competitive advantages or divulging insider information.

Some examples of transparency are:

- Share information relevant for the team
- If you know and can't say, say so
- If you don't know or have the information, say so
-

- Practice "we all know, what we all know"

uncluttered.

The saying I've heard many times is to be aware of those who keep the water muddied because they don't want the rocks at the bottom to be visible. Keeping the water muddied is a strategy used by those who want to deflect accountability, have self-interest in the outcome of a new strategy or just don't have the business acumen to survive or operate when the rocks at the bottom are visible.

A change in business strategy or optimization can create angst in an organization and as old thinking is challenged, the mudslides start to keep the rocks from being exposed. An effective manager moves the team through the process of settling the water and exposing the rocks. A leader then leads the team through action and resolutions that are critical to the success of the organization.

Uncluttered has some common threads with simple and transparent. The threads are:

- Tell the story with one slide
- Define the relevant metrics
- Establish "we all know what we all know" as an operating principle

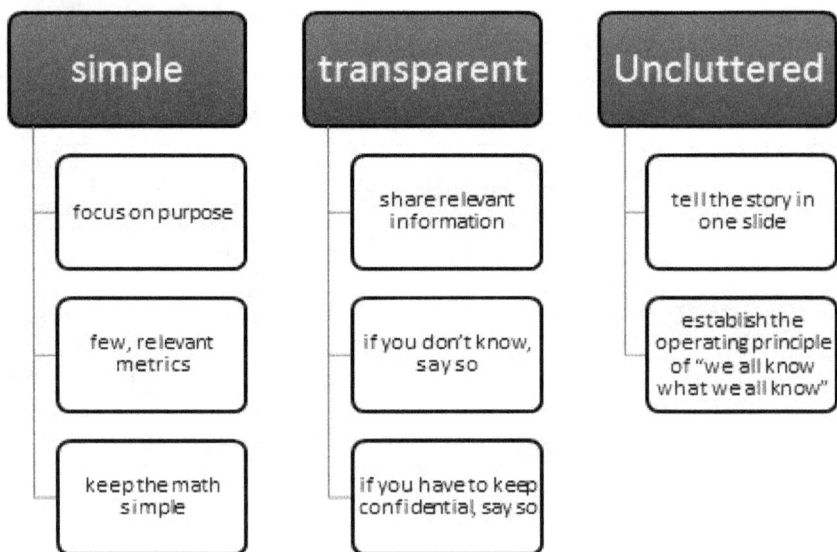

simple
- focus on purpose
- few, relevant metrics
- keep the math simple

transparent
- share relevant information
- if you don't know, say so
- if you have to keep confidential, say so

Uncluttered
- tell the story in one slide
- establish the operating principle of "we all know what we all know"

Chapter Three
Focus on the Fundamentals

people, process, product

In the early 2000's I had the privilege of working at Nike as the finance director for their two Memphis distribution centers. During my first year, NIKE rolled out ten maxims. This was the most effective roll out of corporate vision and values I have experienced in my career. The maxims were the foundation of the culture and business. As in true NIKE form, an inspirational video was the kick off to our guest speaker Jerry West, the former player and coach of the Los Angeles Lakers and by the way, is the basketball model on the NBA emblem.

As one of the formal leaders, I was privileged to present to the Memphis teams the maxim that spoke to me "focus on the fundamentals."

Being the Finance Director, the maxim was close to my heart as I believed and experienced every day that if each of us were proficient in the fundamentals of our roles, the cost of do overs would be reduced, the bottom line would improve and we would all benefit from increased profit. When you focus on the fundamentals, using a management system will provide structure to incorporate all the components that work together to create exceptional results.

The three key components of a management system are:

- People
- Process
- Product

A leader must focus on the fundamentals of each of these categories in order to develop the team and deliver business results.

people

"It" is all about the people. There are thousands of books on leadership and the great ones focus on people. As a new lead, supervisor, manager the most critical element of success for the team and you, is to focus on people. That focus should have *trust* as a foundation between you and each member of the team and trust between and among each of the team members.

I've have observed from a short distance the severe impact to a company's mission and bottom line when there is a severe lack of trust in the executive team by the employees. Each executive leader pitted their team against the other functional teams, corporate wide initiatives that required collaboration were stalled and data was always filtered to shine a positive light on the presenting group, while casting doubt on others. Time was wasted arguing about the filtered data, money was wasted in chasing the wrong problems, and cross-functional collaboration stalled the growth of many mid-level managers.

 If you are managing a process or project, lack of trust manifests in tasks being incomplete due to lack of communication, finger pointing, disagreeing on semantics of the scope of work or sabotage. In production lines, lack of trust is reflected in poor quality and/or blaming the prior process step. Lack of trust is a very expensive problem.

There are many books on how to establish trust, but the simple and most effective is:

- Do what you say you will do
- Treat others how you want to be treated
- Be as transparent as possible in your communications

know your team

Know your team, their individual strengths, their development focus and their individual passions. Feedback is a must in helping your team move forward. The annual performance review is being eliminated in many corporations. GE, under the leadership of Jack Welch, was the benchmark for people development in the '90s and early '00's. The culture of rating and ranking, eliminating the bottom 10% and focusing on high potentials only, is being replaced by immediate feedback systems and playing to strengths of individuals focused on the mission of the team. But, whatever your corporate approach is, you as the leader closest to your team should develop feedback skills that will enhance their development. Don't wait for an annual review or a bi-annual rating/ranking session to have the conversation.

know your numbers
Being a business leader requires you to know your numbers. The numbers are not only the financial and operational numbers, but also your team numbers. Example, how many people are on your team, what the annual cost is for your team, what are the turnover or retention and their key strengths? You never know when you will be asked to take on additional projects or even volunteer to showcase the talent in your team.

process

A large majority of my career was in manufacturing and distribution environments. In those environments, most all team members were aware of what step in the process they fulfilled and what happened before and after their process step, because they each depended on the prior step being completed before they could do their work. But in my experience, "knowledge" based roles seem to have the biggest challenge of understanding how "it" all connects and their individual role in that process. Process knowledge is an inclusive approach that can drive impactful change.

In my finance roles, it was critical to have costs flow to the right accounts, cost center roll ups to the cost center owner and Balance Sheet and Income Statement accounts with accurate balances. I loved the challenge of working with IT on these projects because it was a teaching opportunity for me to help improve someone's business and financial acumen and a chance for me to learn the behind the scenes in IT. Keep in mind that developing your team to not only be functional SME's, but business leaders who are aware of the processes, can impact the bottom line and improve the customer experience. In these days of continuous improvement, cost challenges and quick to market requirements, the more knowledgeable your team is the better the customer experience, the lower cost to service and improved margins will be the result for the company.

Help your team become business leaders by:
- Know the processes
- Share the knowledge
- Continuously improve

product

Being an effective leader means understanding what the value proposition is to the customer who buys from your company and be able to explain the proposition in a simple and concise way to your team and others.

The value proposition could be technology services, sneakers, computers, marketing services or

software. Remember that the service solves a problem or
process need of the customer. But the choice by the customer goes far beyond the product or service—it is the packaging of that service that drives the relationship.

Think of the product as the contents of a box. The contents solve the process or need of the customer, but the packaging of the product can drive long-term value
and is determined by relationship. Simply put, product is the "what and why."

As a new leader, or one in refresh mode, staying aware of the marketplace, competitors and the talent driving change in the industry, are important steps to keeping your current customers, gaining new ones and developing competitive team members.

In "The Profit" on CNBC, Marcus Lemonis, who invests in small businesses uses the 3 P's (People, Process, Product) to assess a potential partnership. Lead your team using this focus and develop your team to be the next business leaders who will attract investment and create great returns!

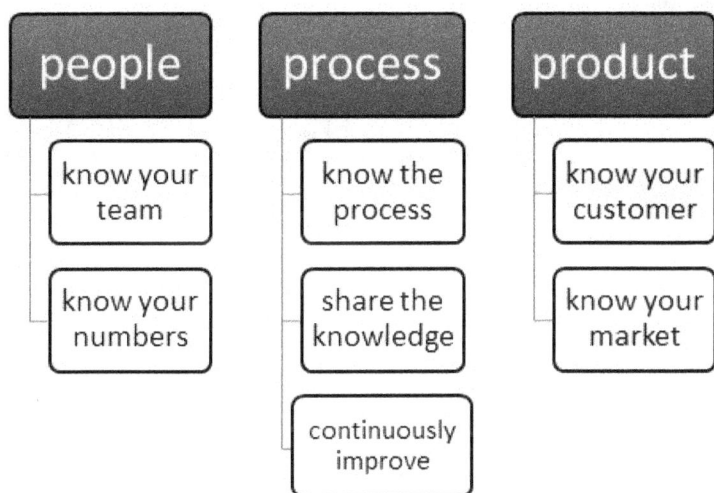

Chapter Four
Staying on Track

work your plan

Business moves at a quick pace with changing priorities, reorganizations, new customer onboarding and leadership changes. But what should not change is the core system you put in place to stay focused and committed to a plan that focuses on people, process and product.

The components of your plan should include:

- Team strategy plan - a review of corporate mission alignment with your team's work

- People plan - team member's strengths and development strategy to support the mission of the company
- Process Plan - high level process reviews that include KPIs
- Product and Market plan - competitor and market analysis

team strategy plan

The mantra of "what gets measured gets improved," can be your driving force in following a plan that is *simple..transparent..uncluttered*. Schedule time on your calendar, include your team in the review and assign review topics to members of the team. Remember, your role is to develop business leaders through getting the work done and delivering innovation!

Team strategy sessions should be engaging, challenge the status quo and most important, require that titles are left outside the room. Transparent conversations that focus on what needs to happen to meet, exceed and morph market requirements, are a necessity for you and your team to share ideas, stay aligned and problem solve. Your team members should leave these review sessions with *simple.transparent.uncluttered.* plans to improve outcomes.

Facilitating interesting and challenging sessions is a key component of transparent communications. Understand that introverts and extroverts have a very diverse way of engaging in idea sessions. The strategy session agenda is the guide. Use a formal agenda, with topics, owners, start time, stop time, breaks and formal wrap up. An effective method to ensure maximum participation is to assign pre-work that could mean reading or topics to be discussed. This will support the introverts on your team to think through their ideas and input and also support the extroverts in formulating a thought through idea versus competing for air -time during the strategy session. Introverts are turned off when the entire session is rapid fire brainstorming with no "thought time." Extroverts can be successful at moving agenda's along. Assign agenda topics to individuals such as a high level review of a competitor, interesting trends from a business journal, high-level demo of new software to provide an opportunity to improve presentation skills or public speaking. Inviting an internal customer to share their wins/challenges will also support cross-functional engagement. The strategy session is to align your team and develop them as leaders. Ensure they are more informed, engaged and excited when they leave!

people plan

The core of our responsibility as leaders is to serve and develop others while accomplishing the objectives of the organization. I'm a firm believer in playing to individual strengths however, there are fundamental skills and knowledge leaders are responsible for developing in their team which requires an intimate understanding of each of your team member's strengths and areas for development.

The development plan should be created with your direct report. This is a plan that addresses strengths and areas of opportunity with *simple..transparent..uncluttered* assignments that will expand knowledge and experiences. These plans are their roadmap to being a well-rounded business leader while emphasizing the individual strengths that make them an exceptional performer. Your follow through on creating the environment and their follow through on the action, is a very critical component of building a trusting relationship that is required for successful leaders. Don't miss these sessions!

During succession planning discussions with your peers and other executives about your team these discussions can go awry when executives use ulterior motives to derail or accelerate individuals within an organization. Be mindful that feedback from others is a real insight into what they value and how they see the world. Know that feedback is not absolute, but another's perspective. Listen to others with an open mind and always be cautious.

process plan
"What gets measured gets improved." I've used this phrase many times, in

many environments and it has always held true! The simplicity of this statement can be understood by your team and let's face it, the person/team who has the data *and* can tell the story in a concise and effective manner, can change the direction!

The process sessions should focus on the KPIs that measure are we getting "better or worse" in the eyes of our customer and shareholders. It is as simple as that.

In order to determine better or worse, the definitions, data collection and calculations of the KPIs, must be in alignment with the customer agreements or expectations. If you are only measuring against your expectation and not your customers, you will soon find yourself without customers.

In the distribution world, time to customer and complete orders are important KPIs. The cost of distribution, directly to a customer door is a major cost to these organizations. Amazon is addressing this KPI by starting their air fleet and drones! If a commercial customer expects their shipment of five items by next day and all in the same box, and you ship 4 items the next day and 1 box two days later, you have failed. The customer now handles two boxes, makes two internal deliveries, manages two packing lists, or two EDI transactions. Put yourself in your customer's position and insist your suppliers do the same for you!

Review the KPIs on a cadence with your team and keep the scorecard visible for the entire organization. Encourage cross-functional reviews, and problem solving and celebrating. Remember, if the entire organization is aligned around the same mission, with the same KPIs, it is a powerful culture that will win and keep customers.

product and market plan
I admit it, in some of my roles I was too focused on developing my functional expertise that I didn't take a high interest in the market of not only the overall business, but in some cases the external shift and trends in my functional area. I was too focused on

the day-to-day execution, staying in the weeds and ignoring the forest and the changing landscape. Don't do what I did!

Keep your knowledge of the industry fresh and all encompassing. Assign your team to research and present it in staff meetings, invite others from different functions in the organization to share knowledge. Be the catalyst to encourage information sharing. Meet with your customers, go see the product or service being used and stay connected!

The business landscape changes at a rapid pace. Don't stick your head in the sand and ignore it and hope it all turns out! Shine the light, engage your team, and create opportunities for sharing information with your internal and external customers.

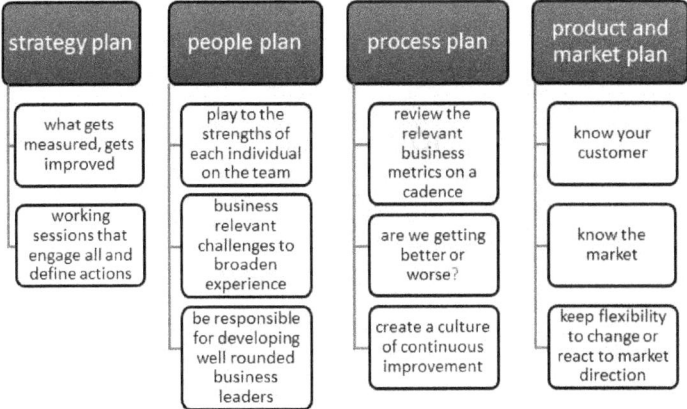

strategy plan	people plan	process plan	product and market plan
what gets measured, gets improved	play to the strengths of each individual on the team	review the relevant business metrics on a cadence	know your customer
working sessions that engage all and define actions	business relevant challenges to broaden experience	are we getting better or worse?	know the market
	be responsible for developing well rounded business leaders	create a culture of continuous improvement	keep flexibility to change or react to market direction

Chapter Five
Moving Forward

be the leader you wish you had

There are enormous amounts of written material you will read during your leadership journey. Some of the material will resonate and challenge you to think about the paths you take, how to motivate others and your emotional intelligence as you take this journey and some material will not. The writings of Simon Sinek and Ram Charan connected with me.

Both Simon Sinek and Ram Charan's writing style and storytelling are *simple..transparent..uncluttered* messages that challenge me to continue my journey of continuously developing my emotional intelligence, asking questions from a curious voice instead of fact-finding voice and developing the business acumen of others. Simon Sinek penned the phrase, "*Be the Leader You Wish You Had,*" and on so many levels this is applicable to life.

You know from where your life journey began, others don't. Your family, neighborhood, school, friends and the experiences you have had. In reflection, there were personal events I experienced a leader who connected with me, focused on my strengths and supported me in my journey that has contributed to the person I am today. I have also experienced a leader whose approach was distant, publicly admonished others and myself on the team and tried to block my journey. Decide for yourself who you are and be the leader you wish you had.

Leadership is a rewarding journey. The rewards are measured in the lives that are expanded, nurtured and challenged, not only theirs but yours! Be a player, a team captain and a coach!

Enjoy the journey!

Remember

Being a leader is a privilege and responsibility so remember:

- It is no longer about you, it is about the team!
- Player, team captain and coach are all important roles
- Master the fundamentals of the role you play
- *Simple..transparent..uncluttered* approach gets results
- Focus on People, Process, Product
- What gets measured, gets improved
- Be the leader you wish you had

Recommended Reading

- *What the CEO Wants You to Know* by Ram Charan
- *What Got You Here Won't Get You There* by Marshall Goldsmith
- *Leaders Eat Last* by Simon Sinek
- *Start with Why* by Simon Sinek

About the Author

Kathleen Winter is the principal at Winter Consulting, her independent business-operations consulting practice. Her practice focuses on helping businesses optimize results using a *simple.transparent.uncluttered.* approach.

Kathleen worked for over two decades in corporate America, in finance and supply-chain roles. In this book she shares her leadership experiences from Nike, Dell, Thomas & Betts, Lucite, and Miraca Life Sciences, advocating a strategic leadership foundation that is *simple.transparent.uncluttered.*

Kathleen grew up in Southern California in an economically poor family. She is a proud product of the California public school system, with a BS in business from the University of Redlands. She started her business career in Houston, Texas, and has enjoyed living throughout the southern United States. While developing her career, Kathleen obtained an MBA from the University of Memphis.

Kathleen is currently living in the wine country of Southern California while she writes and works on business endeavors. She is interested in learning about your

simple.transparent.uncluttered. journey.

Winter Consulting

PO Box 836

Aguanga, CA 92536

www.kathleenwinterconsulting.com

email:kathleen@kathleenwinterconsulting.com

www.ingramcontent.com/pod-product-compliance
Lightning Source LLC
Chambersburg PA
CBHW050540210326
41520CB00012B/2651